RHYTHM of
My Soul

RHYTHM of *My Soul*

A Book of Poems

TAPATI BHAUMIK

Rhythm of My Soul

Copyright © 2019 by Tapati Bhaumik. All rights reserved.

No part of this publication may be reproduced, stored in a retrieval system or transmitted in any way by any means, electronic, mechanical, photocopy, recording or otherwise without the prior permission of the author except as provided by USA copyright law.

The opinions expressed by the author are not necessarily those of URLink Print and Media.

1603 Capitol Ave., Suite 310 Cheyenne, Wyoming USA 82001
1-888-980-6523 | admin@urlinkpublishing.com

URLink Print and Media is committed to excellence in the publishing industry.

Book design copyright © 2019 by URLink Print and Media. All rights reserved.

Published in the United States of America

ISBN 978-1-64367-816-0 (Paperback)
ISBN 978-1-64367-815-3 (Digital)

15.08.19

To my loving daughters Tanya and Munia

Introduction

I am a poetry lover from a very young age. I love to read and recite variety of poetries. Life is meaningless to me without art and poetry. This is my first book of poems. My poems are a true reflection of my philosophy. These poems are written to express my feelings and concerns about this world. I believe we are one family on this planet. We may have different ways of life, but our goal is to nourish and nurture the souls by giving our best to one another. I hope you enjoy these poems. There is a joy in sharing. I could not be a poet today without the support of my younger daughter Munia who enrolled me to a poetry class at the Berkley Extension Course. I also want to thank my older daughter Tanya and my sun-in-law Sujit for their support and encouragement. I would like to thank my beloved husband Ashish Bhaumik for helping me to prepare this manuscript and for his constant support.

Contents

Devotional Poems
- Sri Ma 13
- Rhythm of My Soul 14
- Reflection 15
- Heavenly Patches 16
- My Mother 17
- Salutation 18
- Dream 19
- Salutation to Lord Buddha 20
- Surrender To Final Call 21

Poems on Nature
- Behind Fall Colors 25
- Winter Foliage 26
- Life is Beautiful 27
- Precious Smile 28
- Majestic Nature 29
- Blue Ravine 30
- Dawn 31
- Elixir of Nature 32
- Serene Mother Earth 33

Love Poems
- Up-Close Mississippi 37
- Cruise To Alaska 38
- Summer Night 39
- Love is Lovely 40
- My Valentine 41

Other Poems
- Be Truthful 45
- Father's Day 46
- Last Sunset 47
- Salute To An Everlasting Soul................................. 48
- Trash Can 49
- Unforgettable 50
- Untold Pain 51
- Hope 52
- Divided Soul 53
- Fall Behind Serenity 55
- Beauty In My Back Yard 56
- Folsom 58
- Arranged Marriage 59
- Precious Soul 60
- Loss of a Dear One 61
- Our Love 62
- Depression 63
- Mirror and Me 64
- Untouched Maiden 65
- Uninvited Guest 66

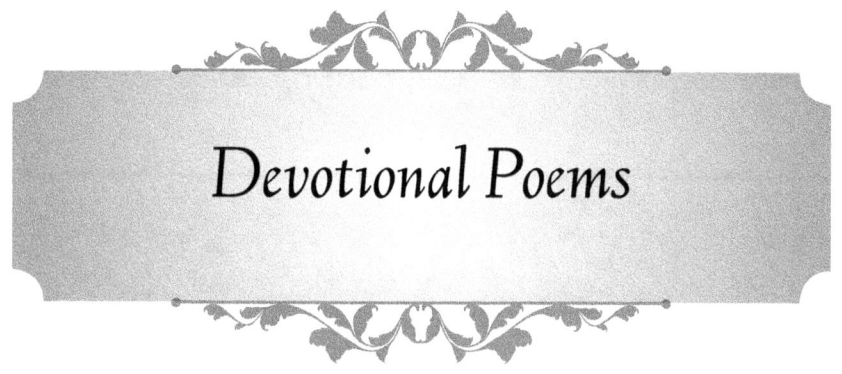

Devotional Poems

Sri Ma

My dear mother as I look at your kind serene face
My heart is filled with joy touched by your grace
Your motherly heart filled with love and compassion
Knows no bounds showers blessings in all directions
You do not discriminate your children short or tall
Emanate love and kindness for one and all.

I bow my head at your feet on your birthday celebration
I feel your presence in this universe of constant rotation
I know your crystal clear spirit is present in every particle
To watch over us in water earth and sky of endless circle
Even now your blessings bring us all together
To make us realize the meaning of life better.

If I can practice very little of your lesson
This says "love the world with kindness and reason
See what is wrong in you and work towards perfection
Instead of seeing fault in others action"

Rhythm of My Soul

I do not have the eyes to see you
Yet I feel your presence in my heart
You create me everyday
You give me strength and wisdom
You are with me in my sorrows and happiness
You transform my sorrows into compassion
I can feel other's sadness.

I hear your footsteps
When sitting quietly
Morning daylight is sweet
Songs of the silver waves are joyous
Soft floating clouds are serene
Quiet murmur of the sea breeze
Uplifts my soul
You are there for me in everyway
Your divinity is at work
I see you when closing my eyes.

Reflection

Holy golden temple on a hilltop
Stands out under the blue sky
Reflecting from the clear lake
Water attracts
White clouds gather closer
Light reflects like a flying bird
Creating illusion of Heaven
Temple shines bright
This unparalleled scene absorbs my mind
Does a magnificent architecture
Welcome humanity or
Divide?
A church, temple, mosque
Is there a difference?
All are beautiful inside or
One creates chosen people
When a temple of love and compassion
Will welcome us as one
Minds will be glowing like gold
Holding hands reaching out

Heavenly Patches

Heavenly patches
God's call reaches my dull soul
Illuminates me.

I look for him
I look up in heaven
I look down on earth

He quietly says
I live within you
Wake up

My Mother

A beautiful petit lady
Dressed in simple manner
Wearing a beaming smile like a fresh rose
Her smile takes away all our pain
Its like calm waves of a turbulent sea
You are not there for me today
But your spirit is present in
Every particle of my soul that came from you
You taught me to love the world with kindness
You gave me the strength to go forward
Your lessons are my lessons as a mother
I bow my head for teaching me things right
Let my vision be just and pure
By your immortal spirit of love
Our beautiful moments together are
Like pages of an unforgettable journey
written in everlasting ink
in the memory book of my life.

Salutation

Have you seen her?
She stands tall amongst millions
She is thin but strong
She is majestic like a piece of Granite
Standing still for many years
She takes the pain of rough weather
She protects her family
She is the mother of all near and dear.

She is tough outside
Sweet and soft inside like a coconut
Loves everyone dearly
She lives by her values and principle
An example of courage
She has a special place in my heart
A loving mother
I salute her with deep respect.

Dream

Last night was different than others
I was captivated by its intensity
It brought out an eternal truth
Lies deep down in our heart
Vivid dream unveiled death
I embraced death as a dear friend
Crimson fire encircled my body
I am transformed into ashes
Giving back myself to the earth
So lovingly held me for years
I am not separated from you
My soul is everlasting in you.

Salutation to Lord Buddha

Oh great noble soul
You came on a full moon day
To illuminate humanity
Lead to path of liberation.

Oh compassionate face
Your realization of ultimate truth
Sitting under the banyan tree
Brought a new light to the World.

Oh great humanist
You renounced your kingship
To love common people
Today you are the king in every heart

Oh gracious Lord
I bow my head to your feet
Bless me
To be fearless of earthly suffering

Surrender To Final Call

Tonight I am ready
Receive me in your loving heart
I am free from bondage
Flying through the floating clouds
Listening to the whisper of the wind

Dear Mother Earth
I spent many years of joy and sorrow
In your unconditional love
You gave me rare gifts
Roses to love and care

Your serene bare blue sky
Your silver rays of silent morning
Made me forget my pain
My soul rejuvenated
Spreading music of hope

Many precious memories
Many faces of love and friendship
All I carry with me
I salute thee with deep gratitude
As I bid good bye

Poems on Nature

Behind Fall Colors

Lost amidst the innocent woods
Leaves embracing each other
Dressed in pink, gold, red, and yellow
Still water of the lake reflecting a dreamland.
Serene Sky is colorful in pastel shades
A picture gallery
Nothing but the touch of fall
An enchanting beginning.
I am awakened to capture nature's gift
It rejuvenates my dull soul
Attracts me like the charm of a young woman
My body and soul lost in ecstasy.
Gentle breeze touches my cheeks
Like soft romantic kisses
Dewdrops on the green grass
Look up to my adventure in wonder.

Winter Foliage

Winter foliage
Playful child adventurous
Creator's gift attracts.

His creation
Blue sky soft breeze
Green pastures.

Let this child
Live within us
Do not loose God's gift.

Life is Beautiful

Sky in pastel shades
Welcome delightful spring
Life is beautiful.

Flowers are blooming
Birds are chirping
Life is beautiful.

Winter disappears
New life comes to earth
Life is beautiful.

Nature's unique painting
Reflects soft tranquility
Life is beautiful.

Precious Smile

A precious smile
Sunflower talks to her
He observes unity.

A smile can win
The unknown world
Bring distant closer.

Let us all smile
No matter how hard life is
Smile is a precious gift.

Majestic Nature

Nature's majesty
Permeates divine glory
Brings tranquility.

High mountains
Silver waves of moonlit night
Soothes our soul.

Love and care nature
She nourishes us
As we come and go in her arm.

Blue Ravine

Blue ravine flows behind my backyard
Melodiously
Carrying an unknown tune.
Tall green grass
Slanted dogwood trees dressed in pink
Reflect from her mirror of water.
She is my sweet love
Lovely in her quietness
I can't miss her a day.
Water attracts
Mystic wind follows me
Jealous to get her attention.
I walk close to her inner self
her endless futile ripples
Resonates love.
Blue crane Rufus twee busy geese
Flickering their wings happily
All find solace in her bosom.
She is my elixir of life
After a dry day of loneliness
She rejuvenates me for tomorrow.

Dawn

Nature's first golden ray
Curved its way
Morning sky is delighted
It's a magic touch
Bright orange covers the skyline
Crimson sun dances in joy
Skylark soars high in the sky singing
To an unknown horizon
An enchanting new beginning of a day
We toil for triumph and failure
You create us again today.

Elixir of Nature

River flows downhill
Rushing out to embrace the world
Loud harmonious voice
Waking up the quiet forest from dreaming
To announce its appearance
Twirling whirling water passes by
Carrying the tale of eternal "human saga"
One end of the world to the other
I wonder how the foils of my life story
Transformed to the unknown
Sun's magic touch livens the water
White spectacular foams forming
Futile bubbles of endless joy
The water evaporates in the air
Will shower upon us in its outburst
Nothing is lost in the universe
Divinity is here.

Serene Mother Earth

Snow flakes are falling down
Like pure white Jasmine petals
As if God's blessings
Reaching Earth's soul.
Everything turns to white
Mother Earth dressed in
Soft White attire
She is rejuvenated.
Her flawless meditating mood
Brings peace on Earth
Quietly I surrender myself
At her lotus feet.
I have seen her in many ways
But this new look changes
The busy world
To a restful cozy nest.

Love Poems

Up-Close Mississippi

Sun slowly setting over the Mississippi River
Golden, orange, crimson reflecting
Nature's majestic canvas spreads on water
Boat carrying longing souls
Softly in slow motion
Music creates romantic vibrations
We all change.
Blue water softens our souls
Lovers' hearts bloom
As we dance, holding hand,
Untold emotions float in each other's eyes
I look at my beloved's eyes
A spark of love unfolds
River has such strong power
That brings out the best in humans.

Cruise To Alaska

A life time desire to
Cruise to Alaska
Two floating hearts
Longing to renew.
Dormant emotions
Hidden beneath
Everyday struggle
Loosing sight.
These few carefree
Days only ours
We are happy as a
Seagull in a sea.
We run around like
Little children
Pouring love and care
Nurturing our soul.
Hubbard glacier watches
Over us curiously
While embracing
Snow hurl very dearly.

Summer Night

Silky summer night
Wind's soft laugh wakes up my soul
Cosmic energy penetrates me.

I see the beauty of dark night
Stars glowing like gold studs
Moon is trying to touch them.

I am romantic
My heart is lost in love
Darkness brings out the best in me.

Love is Lovely

Bright Golden sunlight
Pouring warmth and love onto rivers
A deeper sense of caring.

River is energized
Moving from place to place
Nourishing the earth.

Earth is happy
She wants to give back
Love is lovely.

My Valentine

You are my valentine
When your eyes sparkle
Like the glow of a gentle star
As you look at me.
You are my valentine
When my heart grows tender
As you smile.
You are my valentine
When you embrace me
For who I am.
You are my valentine in
Every moment of my life
Because you and
I are one.

Other Poems

Be Truthful

Knowledge makes life meaningful
Truth makes life simple
Love makes life worth living.

Follow these simple rules
You will be happy
At the end of the day.

You sleep at night
You laugh spontaneously
You live everyday.

Father's Day

A father
A very special person
Sweet memories remind him
How exciting the day was
When he saw his first born baby.

A father is kind and forgiving
Strong as a mountain
Loving like a breath of fresh air
He understands his child
When they agree or disagree.

A father is there for his child
In every possible way
If everyone looses hope
He is the guiding light
When world crushes over his
Precious one.

A father does not ask for return
He does not know how to express
Deep down his child's heart he lives
Lovingly like a calm sea breeze
He is celebrated today with utmost respect.

Last Sunset

As the Sun sets
Sky seems pale
slowly night wraps the Earth
in its black blanket.
Children sleeping
Cozy in their mother's warmth
An owl moving fast
To its destination.
Smashing loud sound
Poisonous gas
Shattered glasses
Screams of helpless children.
What what what?
An attack
Helpless Cry
Help help help.
Last fairy tales
Mother's read
Last sunset
Children watched.

Salute To An Everlasting Soul

No amour can protect us from death
You are now resting in peace
Invisible to your loved ones
Your spirit lives with us.

You are like a gushing river
Ever vibrant and energetic
Waking up the needy and neglected
As you embrace their heart.

You are an example of vision
You are an example of courage
You are an example of love
You live amongst those you loved.

Trash Can

Dark green trash can resting quietly
He is rejuvenated being light today
Every Wednesday he gets a human touch
Even though cleaning person has no compassion.
He does his duty turning him down
The trashcan knows him quiet well
His footsteps are long
He has rough unkind touch
He wonders about this person.
Trashcan starts to get human touch again
He is full again carrying their waste
He gets attention only when they loose
Some valuable possession.
They hug him burying their head upside down
He smiles to their misery
So attached to an object
They turn and toss him upside down
As if he is the cause of all
He stands still
As a context of Modern civilization

Unforgettable

Morning is young
Awaken from last night's emptiness
Skyscrapers are hidden
Gloomy clouds covers the skyline.

Another day of our life
Indifferent souls struggle
Toil for success or failure
I am one of these souls.

Wet surface of pavement
Awaits for human touch
I fell flat on my face hopelessly.

Surprising moment
A wit hard face approaching me
Each wrinkle tells his agony
Loneliness and rejection.

Suddenly he lends his hand
I see God's gift of compassion
His face illuminates in kindness
This will remain with me forever.

Untold Pain

Shadows of Sunlight reflect
Orange Yellow Crimson dances
Small room in a quiet tea garden
Green bushes circles the garden.

River flows quietly beneath the bushes
Carrying the tale of human saga
He grew up in this peaceful soil
Embracing nature's love and beauty.

Suddenly things change
Stillness in the air gives a chill
Morning arrives as gloomy as a
Thick layer of smoke.

He has left
Left for ever
A soul inflicted by
A greedy predator.

Love and peace of nature
Joy of a pure soul
Untouched by human complexity
Lost forever.

Hope

I am tired and empty inside
Looking through the window outside
Gloomy, frail, bleak
Gray veil takes away the beauty.
I try to connect the world
Only news about madness of war
Joyous world dying in despair.
Life shines no more
Human hunger grows stronger
My heart cries quietly
I ask myself, "Who is responsible?"
My inner voice answers
Life is precious and pure
No one cares to nurture and cure
Anger grows into rage of howling tiger
Destroys humanity in senseless outburst.
Let us think to bring back the freedom
For all to walk freely on this planet
Without shooting children.

Divided Soul

Oh almighty time
You appear to disappear
Your eternal circle of cosmic dance
Revolving
Creating and destroying us.

We are lost in your motion
But inseparable memories
Cling to the core of our heart
My mind often revisits a home
I cannot go back.

My beloved home by the paddy field
Soft green grass embracing dearly
An embroidered picture in the front door
Red roses in French knots
Green leaves in cashmere stitches

The door opens to welcome me
Suddenly I hear my mother's voice
As I enter through the front porch
Meaning grows out of that sound
creates our lost days alive.

Wide window by the portico
Attracts me like an old friend
I sit gazing as far as I can
Golden sky shining upon the land
My mind is lost in its charm.

Gradually magic spell of twilight
Covers the land softly in its arm
Evening breeze appears to touch
The joyous dancing strands
Endless ripples follow each other.

As night wraps the earth in its
Black blanket to rest
Earth's soul is calm
My mind goes deep inside
I try to listen to the murmur of the ripples.

Murmur becomes voices of tormented souls
Who cannot go back to their lost home?
Countries broken into pieces
Neighbors become strangers
Friends become foes.

But inner thread of birth land
Can never be torn apart
It lives quietly within our heart
The everlasting hope
Hope of mankind.

Fall Behind Serenity

Lost amidst the innocent woods
Leaves embracing one another wearing
Yellow orange and gold
Still water of the lake reflecting
A dreamland.
Sky is serene in pastel shades
A picture gallery
Nothing but the touch of fall
Morning appears as a dear friend.
Sun grows stronger
Leaves scream
Little Sita thrown
Under jagged rocks
Fall deceives.
Her tired eyes seeking rescue
Gripping branches
Her body invaded by unknown hands
The innocence murdered
Leaves witness
Holding the color of the stain
Lake holds the truth.

Beauty In My Back Yard

My daughter's place is by the lake
In a small Midwest town
I am awaken early in the morning
To capture nature's gift.

I am sitting in the backyard
In a pensive mood
The lake is calm and serene
As if still sleeping.

Lofty blue sky looking upon the earth
Gradually Sun gets stronger
Morning comes with new hope and joy
Struggle of yesterday lost forever.

Folks of swans from unknown zone
Dancing in circles
Plunged in the lake looking for fish
Blue crane watch them.

I see people coming for fishing
Holding hands
They are happier than many people
They are for each other.

Evening brings a different look
Ripples are energized
Sun's warmth pouring on them
Until night wraps them up.

Small boats carrying children
Passes by leisurely
This is a gift of god to be together
In our hasty world.

Folsom

I did not know you
I only knew you are famous for a jail
A singer felt for you
He made you special singing for you.

I have come to you
Now I am closer to know you
You are beautiful
Like a portrait of an untouched maiden.

Fall transforms your woods
To a painted garden of attraction
Your spring brings
Lovely flowers of crimson violet petals.

Your river nourishes
Thirsty souls of thousand birds
You have a gentle manner
Embracing old and new

I love your Sutter street
I love the old town side walks
I love the old America
That you have preserved.

I love you FOLSOM
You are a small lake town
I thank God
For giving me the eyes to see you,

Arranged Marriage

This day was overwhelming
I am giving up everything
My independence and self worth
My family and surroundings.

Anxious moments of expectation
Rapid heart beats are unfamiliar
You do not know your life partner
You are wishing for the best time.

Gorgeous night ready for celebration
Full moon spreads its magic touch
Loud sound of conch shell creates
An auspicious mood of bonding.

I read my vows looking at his eyes
I see two soft romantic eyes
He holds my hands passionately
Assuring his promises in touch.

After many years of togetherness
I reminisce my arranged marriage life
A life of unconditional love and joy
An unexpected friendship.

Precious Soul

Daughters are like special buds
Soft and pretty on mother's cud
They grow as beautiful flowers
Passing by many April showers.

Mother's life is a very busy call
Playing a loving and strong roll
Sometimes short sometimes tall
Trying to stay calm above all.

She cries when comes their sorrow
She laughs as she sees their tomorrow
As they grow she walks side by side
Making sure they could glide.

Her heart grows loving and tender
As they become strong and wiser
They are her best friends forever
Even if life changes to whatever.

Loss of a Dear One

This loss is very sudden
Our hearts are very heavy
A soul so pure and spirited
Tormented in struggle.

We do not live for ever
But if a young soul departs
We are at a loss and dismay
Why did we not know his sorrow?

Let us remember him
A soul full of love and compassion
A soul full of honesty and simplicity
Let's live the sweet memories.

Our Love

She is our dear little joy
She loves to play with toy
She changes our world
We become little children.

We forget our sorrows
We laugh and play
We repeat after her
Whatever she says.

We love her smile
We love her soft touch
We love her dearly
She is a delight.

Depression

Depression is a state of mind
It's not a crime
Those who get depression
Are soft and kind.

The world seems lonely
Everyone talks behind
Loosing their senses
Blaming on you.

Do not give away your worth
Be strong and have trust
Tell yourself everyday
It must go away.

Everything passes by in life
Sorrows and happiness
Rich and poor
Why not depression?

Mirror and Me

I see myself in the mirror
I see my reflection
Fading away, wrinkled skin
Droopy pale eyes.

Tremor that comes and goes
I see the slow motion
I can assess the total physic
The change is true.

Change is a part of the process
I have no regret at all
I have a mind, agile and happy
I want to fly like an eagle.

Untouched Maiden

Darkness outside is deep
Horizon is invisible
Ship moves in slow motion
I try to look outside.

Night's veil of silence prevail
Earth seems lonely
Sweet is the melody of ripples
Heart grows fonder and romantic.

A curious glowing star
Penetrates my soul quietly
I surrender my precious love
An untouched maiden of my dream.

Uninvited Guest

You come as our final touch
You are icy cold
Your shiny wings are too large
You are heartless.

You come quietly in our abode
To steal our life
We are helpless in your presence
We surrender to you.

Your sting is unbearable to us
But we know
You keep the harmony
In cycle of life.

About the Author

Tapati Bhaumik was born in a small town in India. She has a masters degree in Physics and a degree in Computer Science. She is a poetry lover from a very young age. Many of her poems have been published before in different magazines.

www.ingramcontent.com/pod-product-compliance
Lightning Source LLC
LaVergne TN
LVHW021735060526
838200LV00052B/3290